J

MAY YOU ENJOY THIS BOOK

The Public Library is free to all cardholders.
You can increase its usefulness to all by returning
books promptly, on or before the "Date Due"

If you derive pleasure and profit from the use of
your public library, please tell others about its
many services.

THE NASHUA PUBLIC LIBRARY
2 COURT STREET
NASHUA, NH 03060

GAYLORD RG

KANGAROOS

Please visit our web site at: www.garethstevens.com
For a free color catalog describing Gareth Stevens Publishing's
list of high-quality books and multimedia programs, call
1-800-542-2595 (USA) or 1-800-387-3178 (Canada).
Gareth Stevens Publishing's fax: (414) 332-3567.

Library of Congress Cataloging-in-Publication Data available upon request from publisher.
Fax (414) 336-0157 for the attention of the Publishing Records Department.

ISBN 0-8368-4119-0

This edition first published in 2004 by
Gareth Stevens Publishing
A World Almanac Education Group Company
330 West Olive Street, Suite 100
Milwaukee, Wisconsin 53212 USA

This U.S. edition copyright © 2004 by Gareth Stevens, Inc. Original edition
copyright © 2001 by DeAgostini UK Limited. First published in 2001 as
My Animal Kingdom: All About Kangaroos by DeAgostini UK Ltd., Griffin House,
161 Hammersmith Road, London W6 8SD, England. Additional end matter
copyright © 2004 by Gareth Stevens, Inc.

Editorial and design: Tucker Slingsby Ltd., London
Gareth Stevens series editor: Catherine Gardner
Gareth Stevens art direction: Tammy Gruenewald

Picture Credits
NHPA — John Shaw: 9, 13; A.N.T.: 11, 18, 23, 26; Daniel Heuclin: 12; Dave Watts:
    12, 21, 26; Martin Harvey: 14, 15; Patrick Fagot: 16, 17; Rich Kirchner: 19, 26;
    Ann and Steve Toon: 20, 23; A. Warburton and S. Toon: 20-21; Daniel Zupanc: 28.
Oxford Scientific Films — Jen and Des Bartlett: cover, title page, 8-9, 9, 10-11, 15, 17;
    Sally Birch: 6; Patti Murray: 6; Densey Clyne: 13; Alan Root: 19; Daniel J. Cox:
    22-23; William Gray: 24; R. Villarosa: 27; A. G. (Bert) Wells: 27.

Printed in the United States of America

1 2 3 4 5 6 7 8 9 08 07 06 05 04

KANGAROOS

Gareth Stevens Publishing
A WORLD ALMANAC EDUCATION GROUP COMPANY

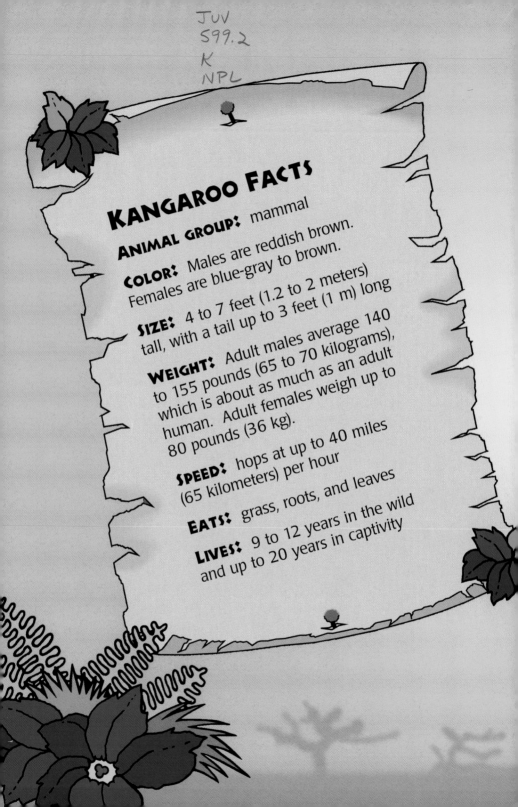

KANGAROO FACTS

ANIMAL GROUP: mammal

COLOR: Males are reddish brown. Females are blue-gray to brown.

SIZE: 4 to 7 feet (1.2 to 2 meters) tall, with a tail up to 3 feet (1 m) long

WEIGHT: Adult males average 140 to 155 pounds (65 to 70 kilograms), which is about as much as an adult human. Adult females weigh up to 80 pounds (36 kg).

SPEED: hops at up to 40 miles (65 kilometers) per hour

EATS: grass, roots, and leaves

LIVES: 9 to 12 years in the wild and up to 20 years in captivity

CONTENTS

Words that appear in the glossary
are printed in **boldface** type the
first time they occur in the text.

A Closer Look

Kangaroos are unusual-looking animals with huge back legs and feet. They are well-known for the way they hop on their strong back legs and for their pocketlike pouches. Kangaroos belong to a group of **mammals** known as **marsupials**. Like all marsupials, female kangaroos hold their babies in their pouches. Some kangaroos are as small as rats. The red, or woolly, kangaroo is one of the biggest. Male red kangaroos are about as tall as a person.

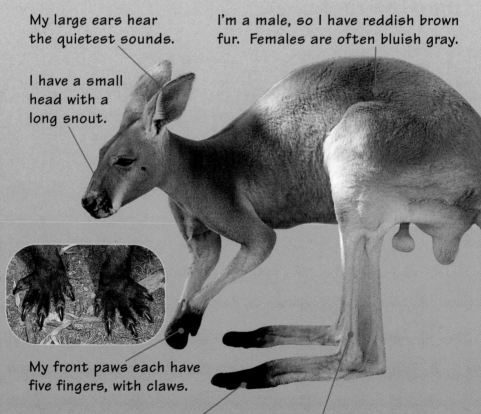

My large ears hear the quietest sounds.

I'm a male, so I have reddish brown fur. Females are often bluish gray.

I have a small head with a long snout.

My front paws each have five fingers, with claws.

I have long back feet, each with four toes that have claws.

My large, powerful, back legs help me hop.

- Australians often shorten *kangaroo* to just "roo."

- A baby kangaroo is called a joey.

- A male red kangaroo is sometimes called a boomer. A female red kangaroo is called a blue flyer.

- Kangaroos are part of a family of animals called **macropods**. The word *macropod* means "big foot."

My long, thick tail helps me balance when I hop and supports me when I sit.

A kangaroo has a small head with a long snout and large, upright ears. It can turn its ears toward the front or the back, so it can hear even quiet sounds from any direction. Its eyes are near the sides of its head so it can see both in front of it and to the sides. Although, up close, kangaroos cannot see things clearly, they can easily see small movements far in the distance. Good eyesight, hearing, and sense of smell help a kangaroo stay out of danger and escape from its enemies.

WHAT'S YOUR SMELL?

Kangaroos make friends by sniffing each other the same way dogs do. Each type of kangaroo has a special kind of smell. Western gray kangaroos are sometimes nicknamed "stinkers" because the large males smell like **curry.**

My eyes are set far apart, so I can see to each side as well as in front of me.

My large ears can hear the softest sounds, and I can turn them from front to back, so I can hear all around me.

My small mouth has thick lips, and my sharp front teeth are great for nibbling grass and roots and for tearing off leaves.

SPIT AND LICK

A kangaroo's tongue is a very useful tool. When a kangaroo is hopping around and gets too hot, it can cool down by licking the skin on its arms with its tongue. As the spit dries, the skin, and the warm blood just below the surface of the skin, begin to cool. The blood moves through the kangaroo's whole body, cooling it down. Female kangaroos also use their tongues to clean their pouches and their babies.

HOME, SWEET HOME

Kangaroos in the wild live only in Australia and New Guinea and on nearby islands. The middle of Australia is a hot desert surrounded by areas known as the bush, or **outback**, which are dry grasslands dotted with small trees. The outback usually does not get much rain, but storms sometimes cause floods. The coasts of Australia are cooler and wetter than the outback. Forests grow in some places along the coasts. The forests of Australia have different kinds of kangaroos than the outback has.

DID YOU KNOW?

European **explorers** were amazed when they saw a kangaroo for the first time. They had never seen an animal like it. They asked an **Aborigine**, or native Australian, what the animal was called. The Aborigine did not understand their question, however, and said "kangaroo," which meant, "I don't understand." The explorers thought that the Aborigine had given them the animal's name, and the name stuck. Now, many Australian marsupials are called kangaroos.

WHERE IN THE WORLD?

About fifty different kinds of kangaroos and other macropods live in Australia and on the islands nearby. South America is the only other place marsupials live. The first marsupials lived throughout most of the world. About one hundred million years ago, they roamed across Earth with the dinosaurs.

GENTLE JUMPERS

Kangaroos have soft pads on the bottoms of their huge back feet. These pads keep kangaroos from stirring up the dusty soil as they leap across the land.

AUSTRALIA

Neighbors

Kangaroos share the outback with lots of other animals. Fierce-looking lizards race along the ground, snapping up insects. Flocks of brightly colored birds gather at **water holes** to feed. They gobble up bugs and seeds or sip the sweet **nectar** of flowers. Packs of wild dogs called dingoes trot around, always on the lookout for a tasty meal. Kangaroos keep out of their way. Dingoes like to eat kangaroos!

Eggs-traordinary

The echidna, or spiny anteater, is an unusual Australian animal. It is one of only two kinds of mammals that lay eggs to have their young. The platypus, which also lives in Australia and is a relative of the echidna, lays eggs, too. Other mammals give birth to live young. The echidna has a long, sticky tongue that is great for gobbling up the ants and termites it likes to eat.

Sun Lovers

Many of the animals that live in the Australian outback rest during the heat of the day and feed at night. But not the emu! This big bird strides across the land in the midday sun. The emu cannot fly, but it can walk long distances on its strong legs. Groups of emus often join each other at water holes for a refreshing drink.

CUDDLY KOALAS

Koalas are marsupials, too. They live in the forests at the edge of the outback. Because they eat only the leaves of eucalyptus trees, koalas smell like eucalyptus, which is a strong scent used in some kinds of cough medicines.

ANIMALS OF THE OUTBACK

BIRDS
Wedge-tailed eagles, parrots, kookaburras, cockatoos, emus, lorikeets, and honeyeaters

MEAT-EATERS
Dingoes and some marsupials, such as mulgaras, dunnarts, quolls, and kowaris

REPTILES AND AMPHIBIANS
Pythons, adders, whip snakes, geckos, goannas, frilled lizards, crocodiles, and desert frogs

ARACHNIDS AND INSECTS
Scorpions, spiders, ants, termites, and beetles

PLANT-EATERS
Possums, kangaroos, wallabies, wombats, and koalas

WATER WIZARD

The thorny devil lizard may look fierce, but it is harmless to humans. Its horns and spikes mainly keep **predators** from attacking. Its spiny skin also helps the thorny devil drink! Tiny grooves carry the dew and rain that fall on the lizard to its mouth.

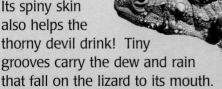

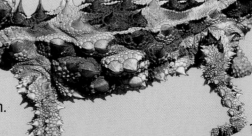

13

The Family

Kangaroos live together in groups called mobs. As many as one hundred kangaroos may be in a mob at one time. A mob often splits up into smaller groups, and kangaroos come and go from mob to mob. Usually, each mob stays in its own living area, or territory. A mob includes at least one adult male along with several adult females and their young. Some kangaroos in the mob act as guards. When danger threatens, they bang their hind feet on the ground, then leap to make the mob scatter.

Newborn kangaroos are tiny. When it is grown, a red kangaroo stands as tall as a person, but it starts out life only about 1 inch (2.5 centimeters) long and not fully formed. A baby kangaroo, or joey, stays in its mother's pouch for up to nine months before it is completely developed. Joeys play a lot. As they play, they learn how to survive. They learn which grass and leaves make the best snacks and how to hide from dingoes and eagles.

IN CHARGE

Male kangaroos can grow to twice the size of females. The biggest or strongest male is in charge of the mob. Kangaroos are usually gentle, but a male will attack if an enemy threatens its family.

Baby File

Birth

At birth, a joey looks like a little pink bean about the size of a child's thumb! Its legs, tail, and other features are not yet formed. The newborn crawls into its mother's pouch and, for the next few months, drinks milk from her body as it starts to grow into a furry kangaroo.

Four to Nine Months

The joey pokes its head out of the pouch when it is about four months old. By about six months old, it is hopping in and out of the pouch and eating grass.

One Year

After about a year, male kangaroos usually leave their mothers and go off to find a new mob. Young females stay with their mothers.

Double Trouble

A joey may drink milk from its mother's body until it is about twelve months old. Sometimes, a younger joey is already growing in the pouch before the older joey is **weaned**. A mother kangaroo can make two different kinds of milk to feed both of the joeys.

Life on the Grasslands

To move across Australia's wide grasslands, a red kangaroo hops. Its body is built for jumping, and the kangaroo can hop for hours on its strong back legs. Its long, thick tail helps the kangaroo turn and keep its balance. Its rear legs work like springs, moving it smoothly from one hop to another. Kangaroos bounce along at about 12 miles (20 kilometers) per hour. At this speed, it takes less energy to hop than to run on all fours like a tiger. When an enemy threatens, a kangaroo can hop away at about 40 miles (65 km) per hour, which is about the average speed of an automobile.

WATER BABY

When a kangaroo is on land, it must move both of its rear feet together. It cannot walk one step at a time the way humans do. To move slowly, a kangaroo balances on its front paws and its tail, then swings its back legs forward. When the kangaroo is in water, however, it can kick its legs one at a time in a kind of dog paddle.

DID YOU KNOW?

- A kangaroo can jump the length of four cars.

- An adult kangaroo can leap about 10 feet (3 meters) high.

- A kangaroo can hop forward but cannot go backward!

FEET FIRST

Red kangaroos travel great distances to find food. Their huge back feet help them bound across the wide outback. The back feet of a red kangaroo can be nearly 20 inches ($\frac{1}{2}$ m) long. Each back foot has two small toes and two big toes. The fourth toe on each foot has a big claw. The kangaroo uses its claws to fight enemies.

FAVORITE FOODS

Kangaroos eat plants such as grasses and the leaves of small shrubs. They nibble the plants right down to the roots. Their sharp front teeth cut stems, and their flat, wide, back teeth crush and grind leaves. They eat the kinds of plants that grow where they live, but they like small leaves and fresh new grass best. A mob needs a lot of food, so the kangaroos **graze** over a large area. They are always on the move to find food, and usually eat after the Sun goes down, especially in hot weather.

JUICY FOOD

Kangaroos love to eat fresh, juicy shoots. They travel quickly to areas where rain has just fallen so they can feed on the new seedlings that spring up.

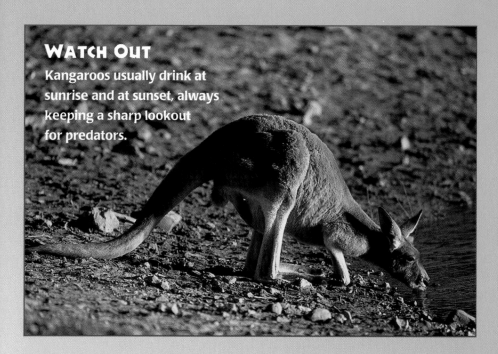

WATCH OUT
Kangaroos usually drink at sunrise and at sunset, always keeping a sharp lookout for predators.

DEADLY DROUGHT

When rain does not fall, plants dry up. If the **drought** continues, many tiny joeys will die in their mothers' pouches. In drought conditions, female kangaroos stop having babies until they can feed on fresh green shoots again.

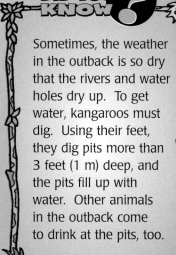

DID YOU KNOW?

Sometimes, the weather in the outback is so dry that the rivers and water holes dry up. To get water, kangaroos must dig. Using their feet, they dig pits more than 3 feet (1 m) deep, and the pits fill up with water. Other animals in the outback come to drink at the pits, too.

DANGER!

Kangaroos are so big that few animals try to hunt healthy adults. Young kangaroos have more enemies. Packs of dingoes watch for joeys that wander too far from their mothers. Wedge-tailed eagles swoop down to snatch joeys and carry them off. Kangaroo guards keep a sharp lookout for dangerous predators, but people are actually the biggest threat to kangaroos, young and old alike.

PROWLING PACKS

The animals that now are wild dingoes once were pet dogs. Thousands of years ago, people brought these dogs to Australia. Some of them left their owners' homes, lived in the wild, and became skilled predators known as dingoes. When dingoes are nearby, a female kangaroo hides her joey in the bushes and leaps away. The dingoes follow the mother, and the joey is safe.

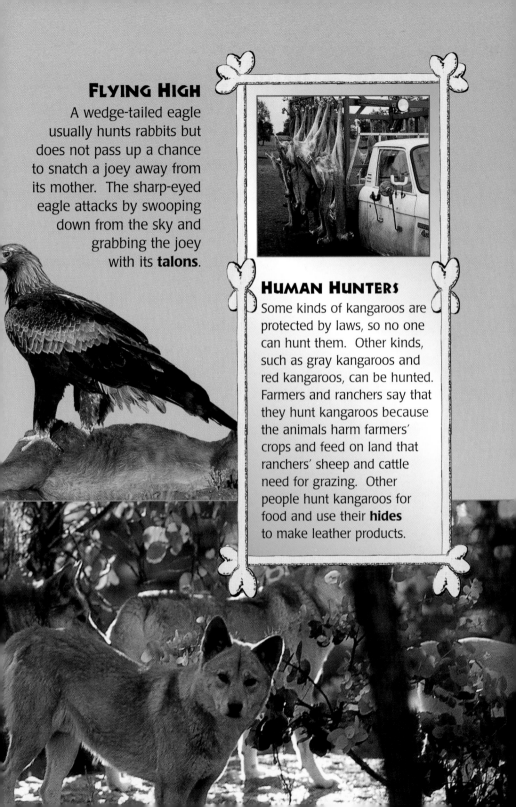

FLYING HIGH

A wedge-tailed eagle usually hunts rabbits but does not pass up a chance to snatch a joey away from its mother. The sharp-eyed eagle attacks by swooping down from the sky and grabbing the joey with its **talons**.

HUMAN HUNTERS

Some kinds of kangaroos are protected by laws, so no one can hunt them. Other kinds, such as gray kangaroos and red kangaroos, can be hunted. Farmers and ranchers say that they hunt kangaroos because the animals harm farmers' crops and feed on land that ranchers' sheep and cattle need for grazing. Other people hunt kangaroos for food and use their **hides** to make leather products.

A Kangaroo's Day

5:00 AM

It was sunrise. Many animals were just beginning to wake up. I took my joey to the water hole and showed him how to find nice soft shoots to eat near the water's edge.

6:00 AM

A male kangaroo that none of us knew came up to our mob. Our large, male leader growled a warning at him, and they started to fight. The stranger lashed out with his front paws, but our leader kicked him with his back feet. The stranger bounded away.

7:00 AM

My joey played with another joey while I fed. The young kangaroos copied the adult males by trying to kick with their back feet and box with their front paws.

10:00 AM

It was getting very hot. We hopped over to some small trees that made enough shade to shelter us from the Sun.

12:00 NOON

The Sun was scorching today. I dug a small hole in the ground and laid down in it. It was nice and cool. My joey slept in my pouch.

2:00 PM

The Sun was very hot on my joey. I showed him how to lick the insides of his arms to cool down.

4:00 PM As the weather cooled, we snacked on some grass, then we took another nap.

6:00 PM The Sun began to go down. I clicked loudly at my joey to call him to my side. We went down to the water hole for our last drink of the day.

7:00 PM We had just started to graze when one of the guards thumped his feet. Dingoes! My joey jumped into my pouch, and we leaped away!

8:00 PM The mob moved to another part of our territory. It rained there last week, so we hoped to find new grass growing.

10:00 PM We grazed on tender green grass. When we find fresh, juicy seedlings like these to eat, we do not need to drink as much water.

12:00 MIDNIGHT At last, it was cool! My joey rested in my pouch, drank my milk, and fell asleep. I took a little nap, too.

4:00 AM The night was quiet. I hope today will be cooler. As soon as the Sun rises, we will go to the water hole for a nice drink.

Relatives

Millions of years ago, Australia was joined to all of the other **continents** on one huge piece of land. When the continents split apart, the animals living in Australia were separated from other animals and developed in different ways. Some groups of animals, such as macropods, live only in Australia and on nearby islands. Gray kangaroos and red kangaroos are the largest kinds of macropods. Kangaroo-like wallabies are much smaller macropods.

Up a Gum Tree

Tree kangaroos spend most of their time high in the treetops. Grasping front paws and the ability to move their back feet separately allow these small kangaroos to scamper from branch to branch.

Rocky Roads

Wallabies are close relatives of kangaroos. Although much smaller than kangaroos, rock wallabies are fast movers. Tough pads on their feet help them run around the rocky areas in which they live. Moving from rock to rock, these wallabies can leap as far as 13 feet (4 m).

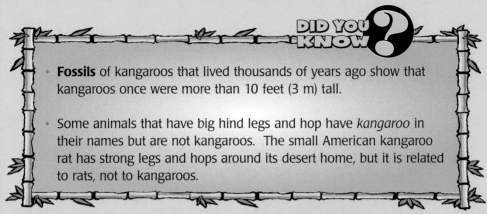

- **Fossils** of kangaroos that lived thousands of years ago show that kangaroos once were more than 10 feet (3 m) tall.

- Some animals that have big hind legs and hop have *kangaroo* in their names but are not kangaroos. The small American kangaroo rat has strong legs and hops around its desert home, but it is related to rats, not to kangaroos.

QUIET QUOKKA

The cat-sized quokka is a type of wallaby. It moves around like a hare in the thick brush where it lives, tunneling out pathways where it feeds at night on grass and leaves.

TINY NAMESAKE

Although the kangaroo rat is a rat, not a kangaroo, it has big back feet like a kangaroo. This tiny creature can go its entire life without drinking water! It gets all the water it needs from the food it eats.

HUMANS AND KANGAROOS

In the wild, kangaroos live in a small part of the world, but people everywhere know them. Pictures of kangaroos represent Australia and decorate that country's coat of arms, as well as its coins, stamps, and souvenirs. This bouncy animal with big feet is a mascot for many sports teams and the star of books and movies. Kangaroos live in zoos and wildlife parks all over the world. Some people even keep them as pets!

HAPPY HUNTING

For thousands of years, Australian Aborigines hunted kangaroos for meat and for hides. The Aborigines painted pictures of their kangaroo hunting adventures in caves and on rocks. Some of the rock paintings are more than twenty thousand years old.

Kangaroos Ahead!

All across the Australian outback, signs warn drivers about kangaroos on the roads. Many kangaroos are killed or injured by cars. Drivers must be very careful to watch out for kangaroos, especially at the times of day when kangaroos are usually moving around.

Did You Know?

- Kangaroos played main roles in *Kangaroo Jack*, a 2003 movie, and *Skippy*, a television series about a heroic bush kangaroo.

- "Tie Me Kangaroo Down, Sport!" was a hit song by Rolf Harris in the 1960s.

- Kanga and Roo are mother kangaroo and joey in the *Winnie the Pooh* stories.

- Australia's Qantas airliners have pictures of kangaroos on their tails.

On Safari

When European explorers first saw kangaroos, they could not believe their eyes. All the zoos in Europe wanted some of these unusual animals that held their babies in their front pockets! Today, kangaroos live in zoos and in nature parks all over the world. In Europe and Hawaii, some of the captive kangaroos have escaped and now live in the wild.

29

Glossary

ABORIGINE
An Australian belonging to the group of Native people who were the first to live in Australia.

CONTINENTS
The seven major land areas of the world, which are Africa, Antarctica, Asia, Australia, Europe, North America, and South America.

CURRY
A strong, peppery mixture of spices used, especially in India, to season foods.

DROUGHT
A long period of dry weather, with little or no rain.

EXPLORERS
People who travel to an unfamiliar geographic area to learn about the area before most other people know about it.

FOSSILS
The remains of animals or plants from times long past, which have been preserved or embedded in rocks and minerals.

GRAZE
To feed on growing plants.

HIDES
The skins of animals.

MACROPODS
Animals belonging to a family of mammals that have very large back legs and long, muscular tails.

MAMMALS
Warm-blooded animals that have backbones and hair or fur on their skin and that feed their young with milk from the mothers' bodies.

MARSUPIALS
Mammals of the macropod family that raise their young in pouches on the bellies of the mothers' bodies.

NECTAR
The sweet liquid in flowers that attracts birds and insects to the plant.

OUTBACK
The harsh, brushy grassland in the middle of Australia, also called "the bush," which has extremely hot, dry weather and where few people live.

PREDATORS
Animals that kill other animals for food.

TALONS
The sharp claws of birds such as eagles and falcons, which are used to grab and hold the animals they hunt.

WATER HOLES
Natural holes or hollows in the ground that hold water.

WEANED
To gradually change from drinking only mother's milk to eating solid foods.

INDEX